DINOSAURS

Step into the world of the dinosaurs

DINOSAURS

Step into the world of the dinosaurs

Original text by John Malam and Steve Parker
Adapted by Jinny Johnson

PaRragon

Bath: New York Singapore Hong Kong Cologne Delhi Melbourne

Consultant: John A. Cooper

Design by Design Principals, Warminster

This edition published by Parragon in 2008

Parragon
Queen Street House
4 Queen Street
Bath BA1 1HE, UK

ISBN 978-1-4075-2602-7

Printed in Indonesia

Contents

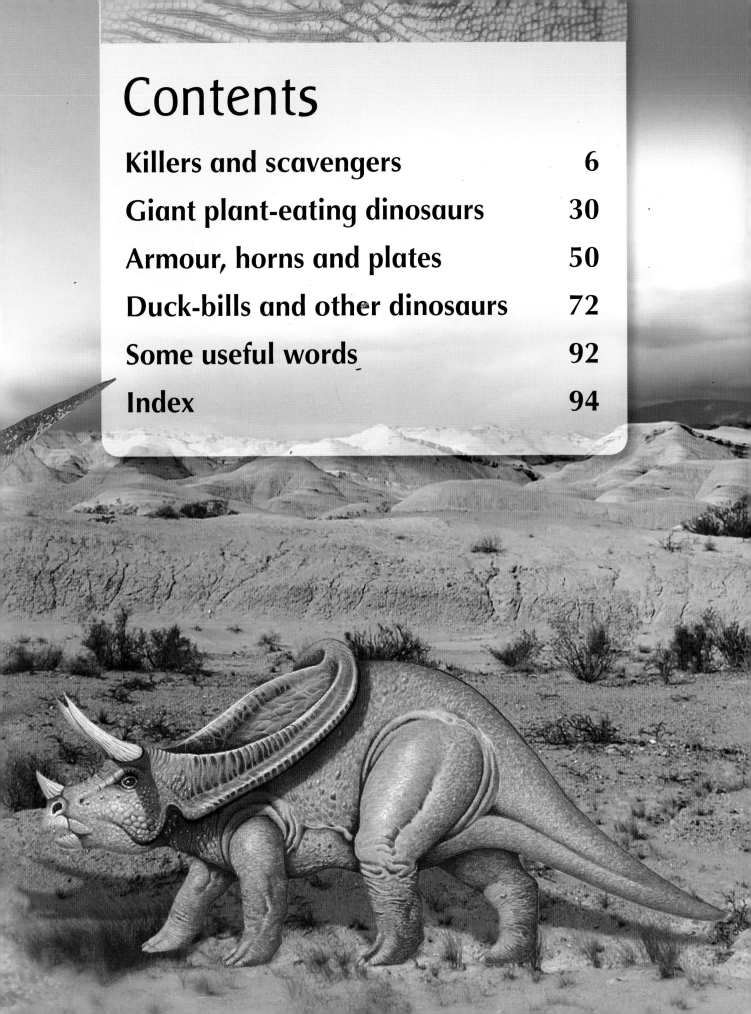

Killers and scavengers

The first meat-eating dinosaurs appeared about 225 million years ago. They included the world's biggest-ever predators. These killers terrorized the world's plant-eaters for more than 160 million years, until all the dinosaurs died out 65 million years ago.

Theropods – the meat-eaters

All meat-eating dinosaurs are called theropods. The name means 'beast feet'. Most of these dinosaurs moved upright on their slender back legs. They could run fast – much faster than the plant-eaters they hunted.

Daspletosaurus

Albertosaurus

Dromaeosaurus

Creature features

Most of the meat-eating dinosaurs had bird-like feet with clawed toes. They had sharp-clawed hands for attacking and holding onto their prey.

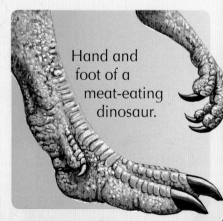

Hand and foot of a meat-eating dinosaur.

Changes over time

Meat-eating dinosaurs adapted over millions of years. Later species were more intelligent and had longer legs and sharper eyes than earlier predators.

DID YOU KNOW?

A *Tyrannosaurus*'s back feet were as much as 1 metre long.

Dromiceiomimus

Troodon

Tyrannosaurus

Dromiceiomimus

Teeth and beaks

Many of the meat-eaters had strong jaws and big teeth. Others had toothless beaks they might have used for cracking eggs.

The first meat-eaters

These dinosaurs first appeared about 225 million years ago, during the Triassic period. They were smaller than later predators like *Tyrannosaurus*, and not such fierce hunters.

Coelophysis

This dinosaur was built for speed. Its leg bones were almost hollow which made it light and able to run fast.

Coelophysis facts

Lived: 220 million years ago

Found: North America

Length: 3 metres

Eoraptor

One of the earliest dinosaurs, *Eoraptor* moved quickly on its slender back legs. It was a meat-eater, but it may have also eaten animals that were already dead. This is called scavenging.

Eoraptor's long jaws were lined with lots of small saw-edged teeth.

Eoraptor facts

Lived: 225 million years ago

Found: South America

Length: 1 metre

Herrerasaurus

Another fast-moving hunter, *Herrerasaurus* had arms that were much shorter than its legs. It held its tail straight out behind it when it ran to balance its weight.

Herrerasaurus facts

Lived: 220 million years ago

Found: South America

Length: 3 metres

Fast movers

Meat-eaters had to be sure-footed as well as fast, so they could turn at speed when chasing prey and still keep their balance.

Going fishing

Some of these small predators, such as *Eoraptor*, may have fed on fish as well as hunting land animals.

Giants

Later species of meat-eating dinosaurs were much bigger than the earliest types. These huge creatures had strong teeth for biting meat and sharp claws for tearing at their prey's skin.

Dilophosaurus

This dinosaur probably moved in groups, searching for prey. The crest on its head may have been brightly coloured and used to attract mates or to signal to others in its group.

Allosaurus

The largest meat-eater of its time, *Allosaurus* was a huge creature with big powerful back legs and a thick S-shaped neck. Its teeth had jagged edges for slicing through flesh.

Dilophosaurus facts

Lived: 190 million years ago

Found: North America

Length: 6 metres

Scavengers

Meat-eating dinosaurs may have been scavengers as well as hunters. This means that they ate animals that had died of old age, or been killed by others. By scavenging, an animal gets a meal without much effort.

Allosaurus facts

Lived: 140 million years ago

Found: North America

Length: 12 metres

Giganotosaurus

This massive hunter was even larger than *Tyrannosaurus*. Its biggest teeth were an amazing 20 centimetres long and could slice deep into the flesh of its prey.

Giganotosaurus facts

Lived: 90 million years ago

Found: South America

Length: 15 metres

Tyrannosaurus

One of the best known of all dinosaurs, this giant hunter lived towards the end of the dinosaurs' rule on the Earth.

Powerful killer

Tyrannosaurus was strongly built and walked upright on its two big back legs. It held its tail out behind it to help balance the weight of its heavy head and chest. It had good eyesight for spotting its prey at a distance.

Surprise attacker

Tyrannosaurus lived in open woodland and often sneaked up on plant-eating dinosaurs as they stood feeding peacefully. It got as close as it could before making a final high-speed dash and pouncing on its prey.

Big head, big teeth
Tyrannosaurus had a huge head, up to 1.5 metres long. Its jaws were packed with 50 or 60 razor-sharp teeth. Some were 23 centimetres long.

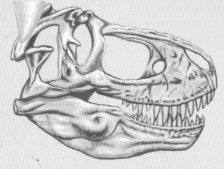

Full to bursting

Like lions and tigers today, *Tyrannosaurus* probably didn't eat every day. If it killed a large plant-eater it would gobble up as much as it could and be satisfied for several days.

Small arms

This dinosaur's arms were so tiny they didn't even reach up to its mouth. But its claws were very useful for seizing hold of prey.

Tyrannosaurus bursts out from the trees to attack a group of *Edmontosaurus* dinosaurs.

Tyrannosaurus facts

Lived: 70 million years ago

Found: North America

Length: 12 metres

15

Spinosaurs

The spinosaur's huge 'sail' was made of long spines covered with skin. The sail may have helped the dinosaur control its body temperature, or been used to attract mates or frighten off enemies.

Soaking up the sun

A spinosaur might have sat with its sail in the sun each morning, soaking up enough heat to keep it warm and active all day long.

Spinosaurus

Like other spinosaurs, this huge dinosaur fed on fish which it caught in its long, toothy jaws.

The sail may have been brightly coloured.

Spinosaurus facts	
Lived: 100 million years ago	
Found: Africa	
Length: 15 metres	

Suchomimus facts

Lived: 105 million years ago

Found: North Africa

Length: 11 metres

DID YOU KNOW?

A spinosaur's big spiny 'sail' was about 2 metres high. That's taller than most adult people.

Suchomimus

This dinosaur had a 1.2-metre-long snout, inside which were about 100 pointed teeth, and an extra-long claw on each hand – just right for hooking fish out of water.

Irritator facts

Lived: 100 million years ago

Found: South America

Length: 8 metres

Irritator

Irritator had crocodile-like jaws packed with hook-shaped teeth for snaring fish.

Baryonyx

In 1983 a fossil collector made a very exciting find. He discovered a giant claw in a claypit in the south of England. Later, scientists found many more *Baryonyx* bones at the site.

Watery habitat

Baryonyx lived near rivers and pools where it hunted for fish to eat. Other creatures such as turtles and crocodiles lived in these waters, too.

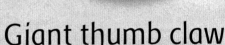

Giant thumb claw

This dinosaur had three fingers on each hand. All the fingers were tipped with sharp claws, and the claw on each inside finger was about 35 centimetres long. All the claws had a tough covering. The name *Baryonyx* means 'heavy claw'.

Long-necked carnivore

Baryonyx walked upright on its back legs. Its head was narrow and it had a long nose, like a crocodile. Most big meat-eating dinosaurs had S-shaped necks, but *Baryonyx*'s neck was straight. Its tail was long and heavy.

Diet of fish

When the first fossils of *Baryonyx* were found they even had the remains of the dinosaur's last meal in the stomach. The remains were of a fish called *Lepidotes*.

Baryonyx snatches a big fish from the water using its long toothy jaws.

Tooth-filled jaws

Baryonyx had long jaws, packed with 96 small sharp teeth. They were perfect for snapping up fish.

Baryonyx facts

Lived: 125 million years ago

Found: Europe

Length: 10 metres

Oviraptor

This meat-eating dinosaur had long fingers tipped with strong curved claws that were perfect for seizing prey.
It may have had a covering of feathers on some parts of its body, especially its arms.

Fierce killer

Oviraptor was a fast-moving hunter. It probably chased smaller reptiles and insects, which it killed with its sharp claws and beak. It may also have eaten some plants.

Oviraptor facts

Lived: 80 million years ago

Found: Asia

Length: 1.8 metres

Caring parent

Millions of years ago, *Oviraptor* lived in desert areas in Asia. It probably moved and hunted in groups. Unlike most dinosaurs, *Oviraptor* took good care of its eggs and may have also looked after its young once they hatched.

Oviraptor skull

This dinosaur's skull was small and light with big holes for its eyes. It had a toothless beak at the front of its jaws and a tall, bony crest on top of its head.

An *Oviraptor* checks its eggs to make sure they are safe.

Nests and hatchlings

Oviraptor laid 15–20 eggs in a little heap of sand on the ground. The dinosaur sat on these eggs to keep them warm until they hatched.

Ornithomimids

These dinosaurs looked very like the big flightless birds, such as ostriches, that we know today. They ran upright on their long back legs and had toothless beaks.

Deinocheirus

Only the arm bones of this dinosaur have ever been found, but experts think it was an ornithomimid.

Gallimimus

When *Gallimimus* ran, it held its long tail straight out behind it to help it keep its balance. This was one of the largest of the ornithomimid dinosaurs.

DID YOU KNOW?

Deinocheirus had enormous claws that were up to 25 centimetres long.

Gallimimus facts

Lived: 70 million years ago	
Found: Asia	
Length: 6 metres	

Deinocheirus may have been twice the size of *Gallimimus*.

Deinocheirus facts

Lived: 70 million years ago

Found: Asia

Length: Uncertain

A mixed diet

Ornithomimids probably ate plants as well as small creatures. Their long fingers and sharp claws were the right shape for digging for insects and plants.

Long, slim legs show that this dinosaur was a fast mover.

Ornithomimus

Like all ornithomimids, this dinosaur could run fast to catch prey and to escape from danger.

Ornithomimus facts

Lived: 70 million years ago

Found: North America

Length: 3.5 metres

23

Dromaeosaurs

All these dinosaurs were very fierce hunters. They had big sharp claws on their feet and strong hands for grabbing hold of their prey.

Utahraptor

The claw on *Utahraptor*'s second toe was 38 centimetres long. The dinosaur attacked prey with these killer claws while holding on tight with its strong hands.

Utahraptor facts

Lived: 125 million years ago

Found: North America

Length: 6.5 metres

Dromaeosaurus

This dinosaur, like other dromaeosaurs, could speed along at 60 kilometres per hour. It had lots of sharp teeth and a large curved claw on each foot.

Dromaeosaurus facts

Lived: 70 million years ago

Found: North America

Length: 1.8 metres

Clever hunters

Dromaeosaurs probably hunted in packs, working together to bring down much larger animals.

Fossils have been found of *Velociraptor* attacking a *Protoceratops* dinosaur.

Velociraptor

Velociraptor had sharp, serrated teeth and a large sickle-shaped claw on each foot. It held its big foot claws off the ground when it wasn't attacking prey, so they didn't get worn down and blunt.

Velociraptor facts

Lived: 70 million years ago

Found: Asia

Length: 1.8 metres

Deinonychus

This meat-eater was a fierce hunter which had deadly claws on each foot. By hunting in packs, it could attack and kill prey much larger than itself.

Speedy hunter

Deinonychus ran fast on its long back legs, holding its tail out behind to help it balance. On its hands were three fingers, each with a sharp curved claw.

Terrible claw

Deinonychus means 'terrible claw'. It got this name because of the curved claw on the second toe of each foot, which could grow up to 13 centimetres long.

Tearing teeth

Deinonychus's jaws were packed with lots of teeth with jagged edges. Some were up to 8 centimetres long.

A pack of *Deinonychus* attacking a large plant-eating dinosaur.

Killer or scavenger?

Deinonychus was one of the top hunters in the area and time it lived in. But it may have eaten animals that were already dead as well as hunting for its own prey.

Deinonychus facts

Lived: 110 million years ago

Found: North America

Length: 3 metres

'Dino-birds'

These small meat-eating dinosaurs looked like birds, with feathery arms and big beaks. They could even use their clawed feet to climb into trees.

Archaeopteryx

Archaeopteryx had feathers like a bird, but teeth and a bony tail like a reptile. It may have been able to fly short distances.

Archaeopteryx facts

Lived: 150 million years ago

Found: Europe

Length: 60 centimetres

Taking to the trees

Like birds, feathered dinosaurs could dart about in trees to find food and escape from enemies.

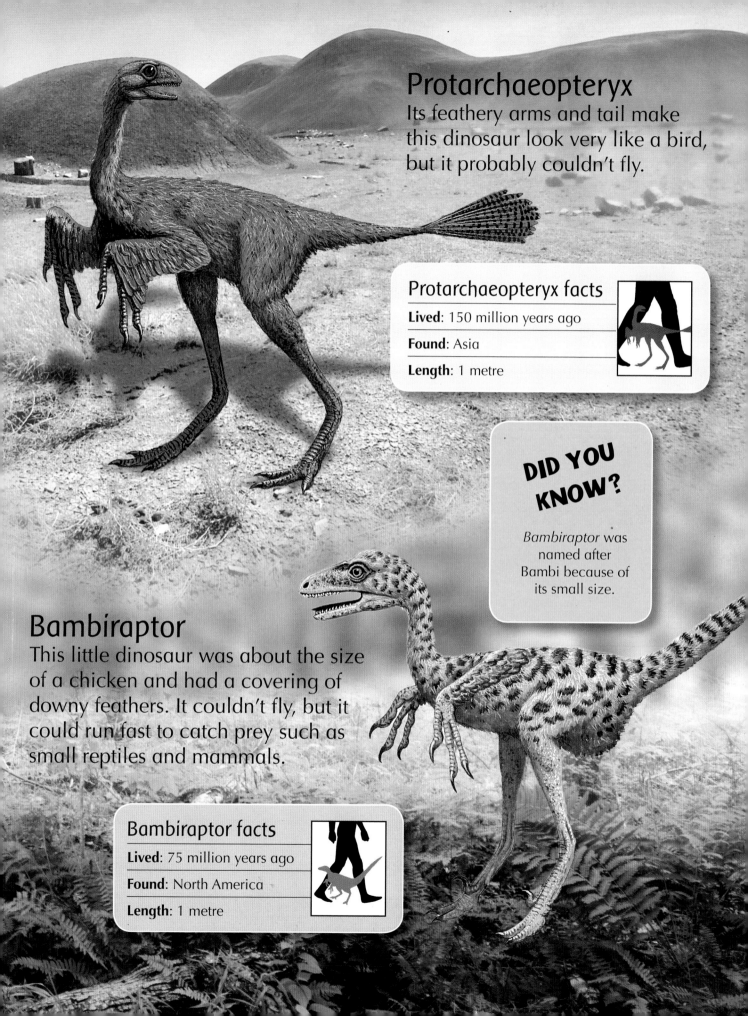

Protarchaeopteryx

Its feathery arms and tail make this dinosaur look very like a bird, but it probably couldn't fly.

Protarchaeopteryx facts

Lived: 150 million years ago

Found: Asia

Length: 1 metre

DID YOU KNOW?

Bambiraptor was named after Bambi because of its small size.

Bambiraptor

This little dinosaur was about the size of a chicken and had a covering of downy feathers. It couldn't fly, but it could run fast to catch prey such as small reptiles and mammals.

Bambiraptor facts

Lived: 75 million years ago

Found: North America

Length: 1 metre

Giant plant-eating dinosaurs

Biggest of all the plant-eating dinosaurs were the sauropods. Experts think these huge long-necked dinosaurs were the largest animals that have ever lived on land.

The sauropods

The first sauropods lived about 220 million years ago and there were many different kinds. The name means 'lizard feet'.

Creature features

Sauropods walked on all fours on their big heavy legs. They all had long necks and tails, but their heads were very small.

Brachiosaurus

Strong legs

A sauropod needed strong legs to support its heavy body. The biggest bones in a sauropod's body were its leg bones.

32

Food for all

Full-grown sauropods could feed on leaves at the tops of trees. Their young ate the leaves lower down.

A herd of *Diplodocus* feeds alongside other sauropods on the river-bank.

Gulping their food down

Sauropods used their teeth for stripping leaves from branches. They couldn't chew properly so just gulped their food down whole.

Big for defence

Being big helped protect sauropods from fierce predators. They couldn't run away fast, but they could lash out at enemies with their long tails.

Camarasaurus

Where in the world?

Fossils of these dinosaurs have been discovered in most parts of the world, but none have been found in Antarctica yet.

Massospondylus

Massospondylus was a typical prosauropod. It had a bulky body, a long neck and tail, and a small head. It lived in the early Jurassic period, before the huge sauropods.

Reaching up

This big plant-eater could probably stand up on its back legs for a short while to feed on leaves high in the trees.

Teeth like pegs

The peg-like teeth of this dinosaur were just the right shape for stripping leaves from branches.

Stomach stones

Some dinosaurs, such as *Massospondylus*, couldn't chew very well. Instead they swallowed stones that helped grind up the food into a mush in their stomach.

34

Tree-eater

The main foods of *Massospondylus* were the needle-like leaves of conifer trees, as well as gingko leaves and horsetail plants.

Thumb claws

This dinosaur had four sharp-clawed fingers on each hand. And there was an extra-large claw on each of its thumbs.

Massospondylus reaches up to eat some gingko leaves.

Massospondylus facts

Lived: 200 million years ago

Found: Africa, North America

Length: 5 metres

Cetiosaurs

These were some of the earliest sauropods. All had a heavy body and a solid backbone. Some later sauropods had bones that were partly hollow, which made them lighter.

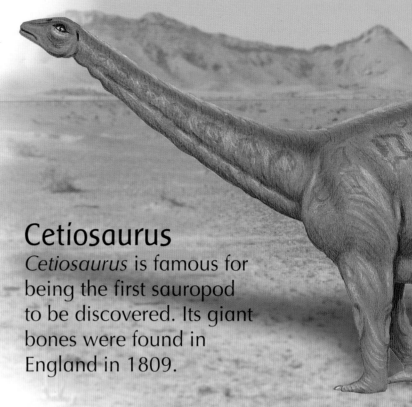

Cetiosaurus

Cetiosaurus is famous for being the first sauropod to be discovered. Its giant bones were found in England in 1809.

Barapasaurus

Barapasaurus had a long tail and neck like other cetiosaurs. Its spoon-shaped teeth had jagged edges for stripping leaves from branches.

Barapasaurus facts

Lived: 200 million years ago

Found: Asia

Length: 18 metres

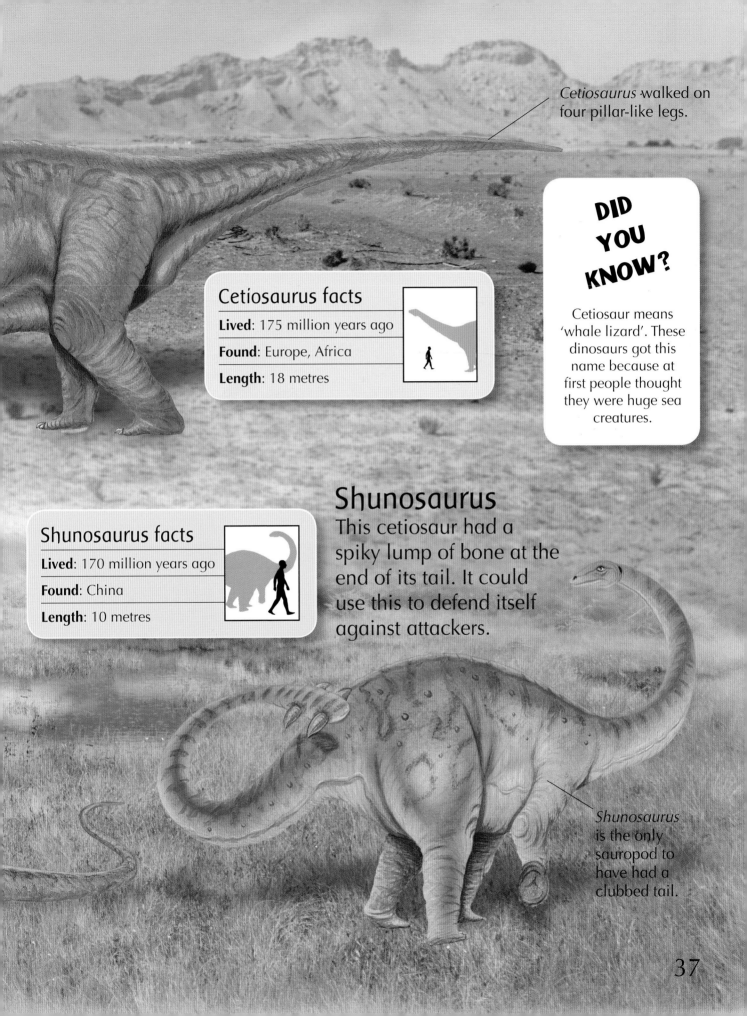

Cetiosaurus walked on four pillar-like legs.

Cetiosaurus facts

Lived: 175 million years ago

Found: Europe, Africa

Length: 18 metres

Shunosaurus

This cetiosaur had a spiky lump of bone at the end of its tail. It could use this to defend itself against attackers.

Shunosaurus facts

Lived: 170 million years ago

Found: China

Length: 10 metres

Shunosaurus is the only sauropod to have had a clubbed tail.

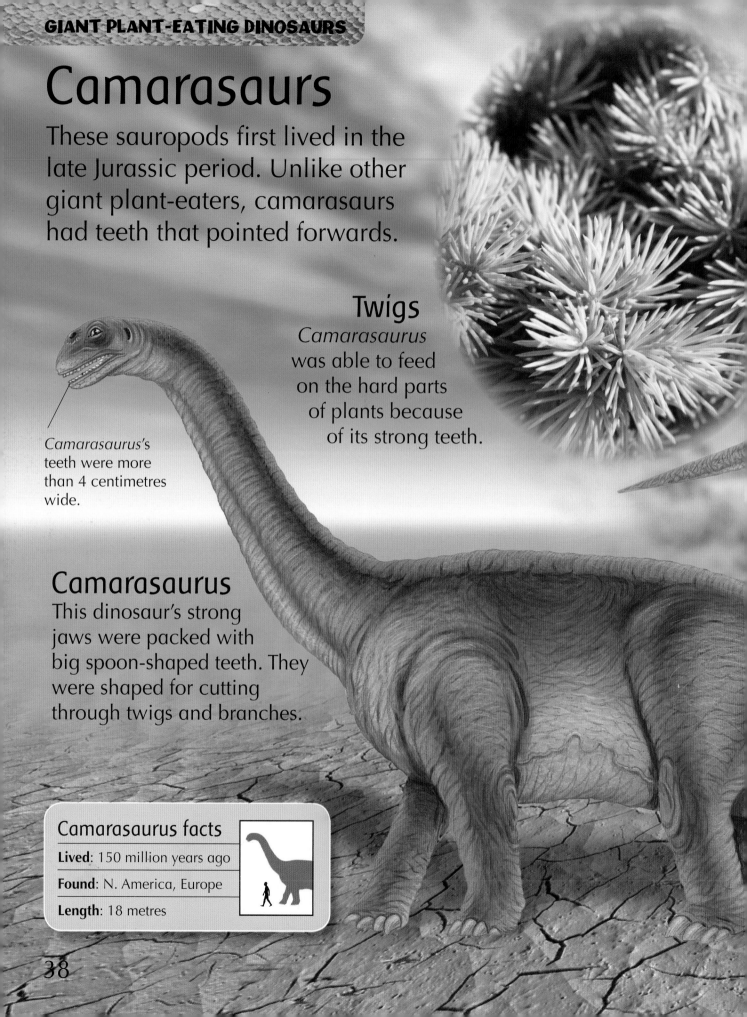

Camarasaurs

These sauropods first lived in the late Jurassic period. Unlike other giant plant-eaters, camarasaurs had teeth that pointed forwards.

Twigs

Camarasaurus was able to feed on the hard parts of plants because of its strong teeth.

Camarasaurus's teeth were more than 4 centimetres wide.

Camarasaurus

This dinosaur's strong jaws were packed with big spoon-shaped teeth. They were shaped for cutting through twigs and branches.

Camarasaurus facts

Lived: 150 million years ago

Found: N. America, Europe

Length: 18 metres

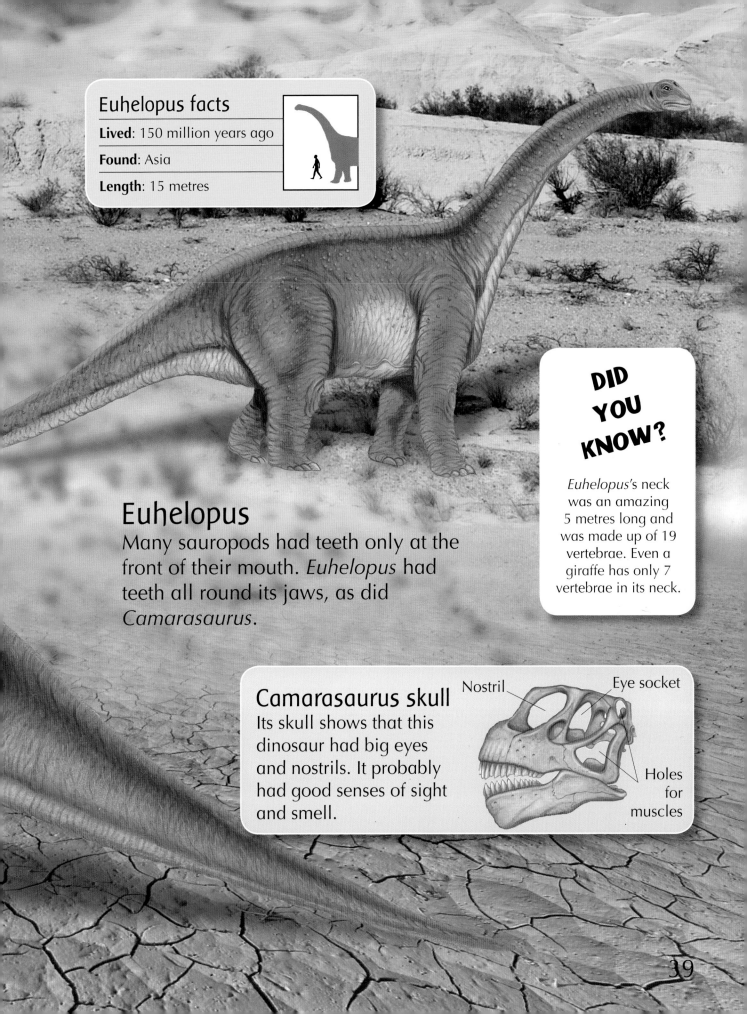

Euhelopus facts

Lived: 150 million years ago

Found: Asia

Length: 15 metres

Euhelopus

Many sauropods had teeth only at the front of their mouth. *Euhelopus* had teeth all round its jaws, as did *Camarasaurus*.

DID YOU KNOW?

Euhelopus's neck was an amazing 5 metres long and was made up of 19 vertebrae. Even a giraffe has only 7 vertebrae in its neck.

Camarasaurus skull

Its skull shows that this dinosaur had big eyes and nostrils. It probably had good senses of sight and smell.

Nostril

Eye socket

Holes for muscles

39

Brachiosaurus

Huge *Brachiosaurus* had an amazingly long neck. This meant it could reach out and munch on lots of different plants without moving far.

A good sense of smell

Brachiosaurus had big nostrils at the top of its head. It may have had a good sense of smell so could smell food and other animals before it could see them.

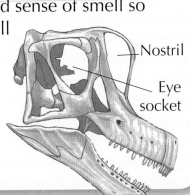

Nostril

Eye socket

Brachiosaurus dinosaurs would have stripped the leaves from trees.

Miniature brain

This huge creature had a small head for its body and a tiny brain. Its front legs were longer than its back legs so its body sloped down towards its short tail.

Living in a group

Brachiosaurus probably moved around in a group, or herd. The dinosaurs would have spent most of their time looking for food and eating.

High and low

Brachiosaurus may have reared up on its back legs to reach high leaves. Or it may have kept all four feet firmly on the ground as it swung its long neck from side to side to find food.

DID YOU KNOW?

A big animal like *Brachiosaurus* needed lots of food. It may have eaten 200 kilograms of plants every day.

Brachiosaurus facts

Lived: 150 million years ago

Found: Africa, Europe, N. America

Length: 25 metres

41

Diplodocids

This group of dinosaurs includes the longest animals that have ever lived on the Earth. There were lots of these dinosaurs in the late Jurassic period.

Mamenchisaurus's neck contained as many as 19 vertebrae.

Tail like a whip
A diplodocid's tail had a long, thin tip like a whip. The dinosaur could lash out against an attacker with its tail. This could cause serious wounds and scare the enemy away.

Mamenchisaurus
This Chinese dinosaur had one of the longest necks of any dinosaur. It made up more than half the animal's length and it measured an amazing 14 metres long.

Mamenchisaurus facts	
Lived: 160 million years ago	
Found: Asia	
Length: 25 metres	

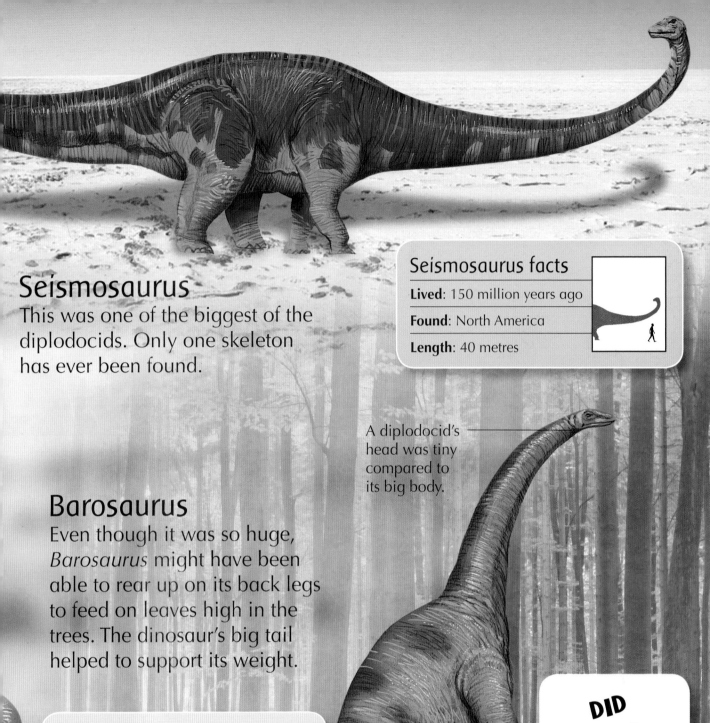

Seismosaurus

This was one of the biggest of the diplodocids. Only one skeleton has ever been found.

Seismosaurus facts

Lived: 150 million years ago

Found: North America

Length: 40 metres

Barosaurus

Even though it was so huge, *Barosaurus* might have been able to rear up on its back legs to feed on leaves high in the trees. The dinosaur's big tail helped to support its weight.

A diplodocid's head was tiny compared to its big body.

Barosaurus facts

Lived: 150 million years ago

Found: N. America, Africa

Length: 27 metres

DID YOU KNOW?

A diplodocid dinosaur could weigh over 30 tonnes, more than the weight of five full-grown elephants.

Diplodocus

This is one of the biggest and best known of the diplodocids. Experts used to think it dragged its tail on the ground. But fossilized tracks show that it held its tail up as it walked.

Fern-eater

Diplodocus probably couldn't lift its head very high. So it may have eaten lots of low-growing plants such as ferns.

10-tonne beast

Although *Diplodocus* was so long, it weighed only 10 tonnes. This was less than some other sauropods. The dinosaur was light for its size because many of the bones in its back were hollow.

Extra bones

There was an extra bone beneath each of the vertebrae making up this dinosaur's backbone. These extra bones strengthened the tail.

Long neck, tiny head

This giant dinosaur's neck was up to about 8 metres long. But its head was tiny. It measured only about 50 centimetres.

Teeth

Diplodocus teeth

Diplodocus had 50–60 weak teeth in the front of its mouth, but no teeth for chewing food.

Diplodocus facts

Lived: 150 million years ago

Found: North America

Length: 27 metres

Titanosaurs

This group of sauropods first lived in the late Jurassic period. Their name means 'gigantic lizards'.

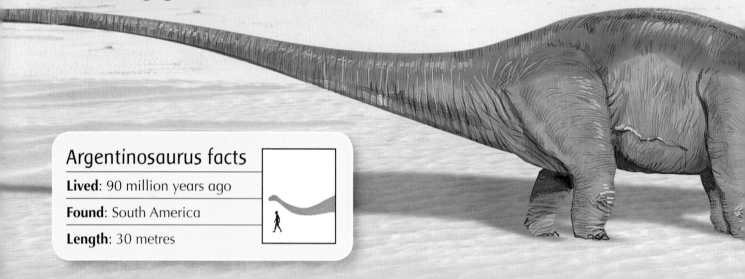

Argentinosaurus facts

Lived: 90 million years ago

Found: South America

Length: 30 metres

Alamosaurus

So far, *Alamosaurus* is the only titanosaur from North America. It lived until the end of the Cretaceous period, 65 million years ago, when dinosaurs were wiped out.

Alamosaurus facts

Lived: 70 million years ago

Found: North America

Length: 21 metres

Argentinosaurus

This enormous creature may have weighed as much as 100 tonnes. Only the biggest meat-eaters, such as *Giganotosaurus*, would have dared attack such a monster.

Body armour

Saltasaurus's back was studded with bony plates, about 10 centimetres across, and pea-sized lumps of bone.

Saltasaurus

Saltasaurus had a long neck and tail like other sauropods. But, unusually, it also had armoured skin that may have helped protect it from meat-eaters.

Saltasaurus facts

Lived: 80 million years ago

Found: South America

Length: 12 metres

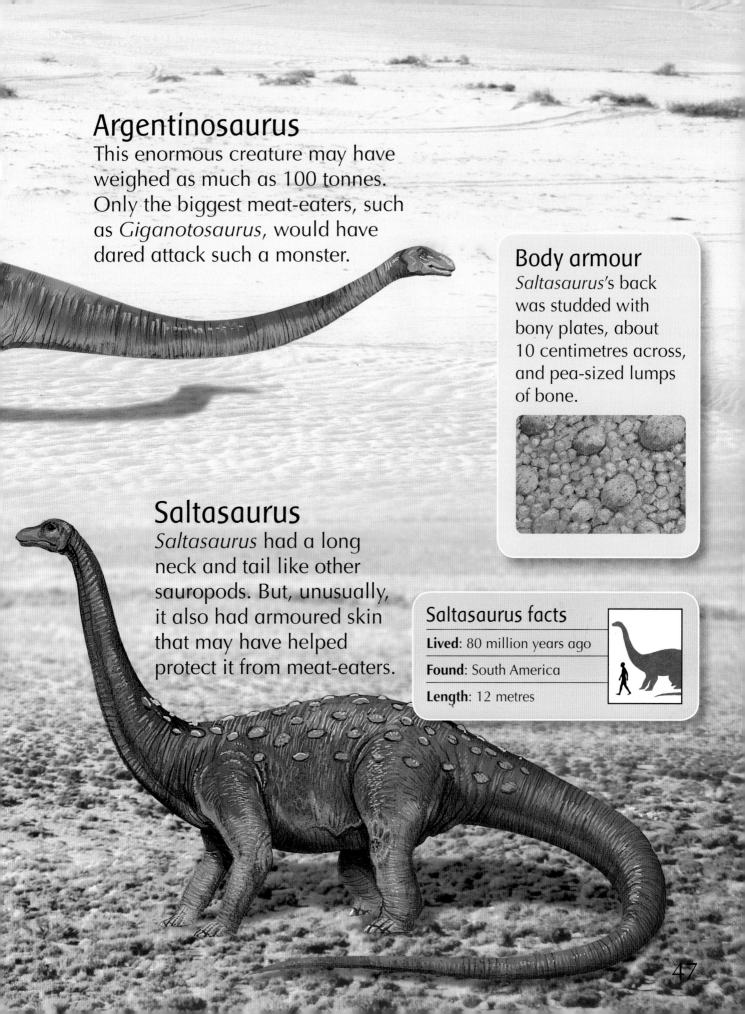

47

Titanosaurus

The first fossil of this dinosaur to be found was a leg bone discovered in India in 1871. Soon more bones were dug up and scientists realized this was a new species of dinosaur.

Naming the new dinosaur

Titanosaurus was named after the Titans in ancient Greek stories. The Titans had great strength and special powers.

A herd of *Titanosaurus* dinosaurs arrives at the river-bank to drink.

Titanosaurus facts

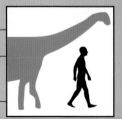

Lived: 70 million years ago

Found: Africa, Asia, Europe, South America

Length: 20 metres

Old and young together

Titanosaurus lived in a herd. This was a group of dinosaurs, old and young, that moved around together. Young animals walked in the centre of the herd for safety.

Stones in the stomach

Flowering plants such as magnolia had started to grow on Earth by *Titanosaurus*'s time. The dinosaur fed on the leaves of these trees and others. It swallowed stones to help grind down the food in its stomach.

Death of a giant

Big meat-eaters usually attacked the younger or weaker members of a *Titanosaurus* herd.

49

Armour, horns and plates

Sauropods were not the only plant-eating dinosaurs. Other kinds included armoured dinosaurs, stegosaurs and horned dinosaurs. They were all smaller than sauropods, but they had their own built-in body armour.

Plated, armoured, bone-headed and horned dinosaurs

All these groups of dinosaurs had horns or other bony lumps and bumps on their body. These helped protect them from meat-eaters.

Spiky tail
Stegosaurs had long sharp spikes at the end of their tails.

Euoplocephalus

Plated dinosaurs
The plated dinosaurs were called stegosaurs. All had rows of large bony plates sticking up along the back.

52

Armoured dinosaurs

This group included nodosaurs and ankylosaurs. Both types had bony plates in the skin and spikes on the body.

Bone-headed and horned dinosaurs

These dinosaurs get their name from their heads, on which were sharp horns or specially thickened bones.

Torosaurus

Stegoceras

DID YOU KNOW?

One of the biggest of the armoured dinosaurs was *Ankylosaurus*, which weighed up to 4 tonnes.

Elephant-like legs

Most of these dinosaurs had thick legs, like those of an elephant. These legs were quite short and stiff but strong enough to carry the dinosaur's heavy body.

Stegosaurs

The first stegosaurs lived about 170 million years ago. There were lots of different kinds and they lived in Africa, Asia, Europe and North America. The last stegosaurs died out about 90 million years ago.

Dacentrurus

This stegosaur had two rows of big bony spikes along its back and down to the tip of its tail.

Dacentrurus had a small head like other stegosaurs.

Scelidosaurus

Scelidosaurus came before the stegosaurs and was related to them. Its body was covered with lots of bony studs that made it hard to attack.

Scelidosaurus facts

Lived: 200 million years ago

Found: Europe

Length: 4 metres

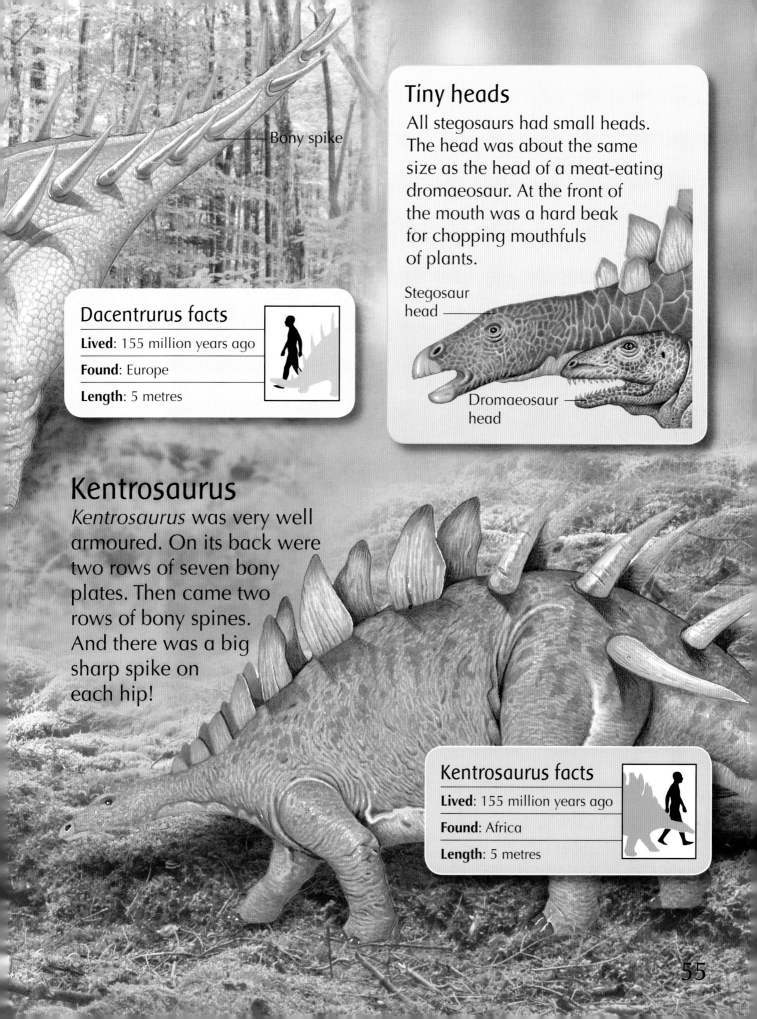

Bony spike

Tiny heads

All stegosaurs had small heads. The head was about the same size as the head of a meat-eating dromaeosaur. At the front of the mouth was a hard beak for chopping mouthfuls of plants.

Stegosaur head

Dromaeosaur head

Dacentrurus facts

Lived: 155 million years ago

Found: Europe

Length: 5 metres

Kentrosaurus

Kentrosaurus was very well armoured. On its back were two rows of seven bony plates. Then came two rows of bony spines. And there was a big sharp spike on each hip!

Kentrosaurus facts

Lived: 155 million years ago

Found: Africa

Length: 5 metres

Stegosaurus

Stegosaurus was the biggest stegosaur. Lots of fossils have been found so it is also the best known of its family.

DID YOU KNOW?

The skin covering the plates on a stegosaur's back may have flushed red with blood when the animal was excited or scared.

Roof reptile

When fossils of this dinosaur were first found, experts thought that the bony plates lay flat, covering the animal's back like a turtle's shell. Because of this, the dinosaur was given the name *Stegosaurus*, which means 'roofed reptile'. Later they realized that the plates actually stood upright.

Sting in the tail

Stegosaurus was a slow-moving plant-eater. It probably moved around in small groups. If attacked, *Stegosaurus* could not run away very fast so stood still and hit out against its enemy with its spiky tail.

Stegosaurus plate pattern

Experts aren't sure how the bony plates were arranged. They may have been in one row, in pairs or overlapping in a staggered row.

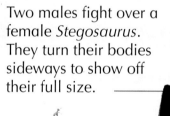

Two males fight over a female *Stegosaurus*. They turn their bodies sideways to show off their full size.

Stegosaurus facts

Lived: 140 million years ago

Found: North America

Length: 9 metres

Nodosaurs

The first armoured dinosaurs were the nodosaurs. They all had lumps of bone set into the skin on their backs. This made them much harder for meat-eating dinosaurs to attack.

Minmi

Minmi was the first armoured dinosaur to be found in the southern hemisphere.

Unusually, bony plates also protected *Minmi*'s belly.

Gastonia

This dinosaur was a fearsome sight. It had big sharp spikes sticking out of its sides as well as bony studs on its back.

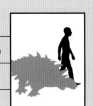

Gastonia facts

Lived: 125 million years ago

Found: North America

Length: 2.5 metres

The spikes were up to 30 centimetres long.

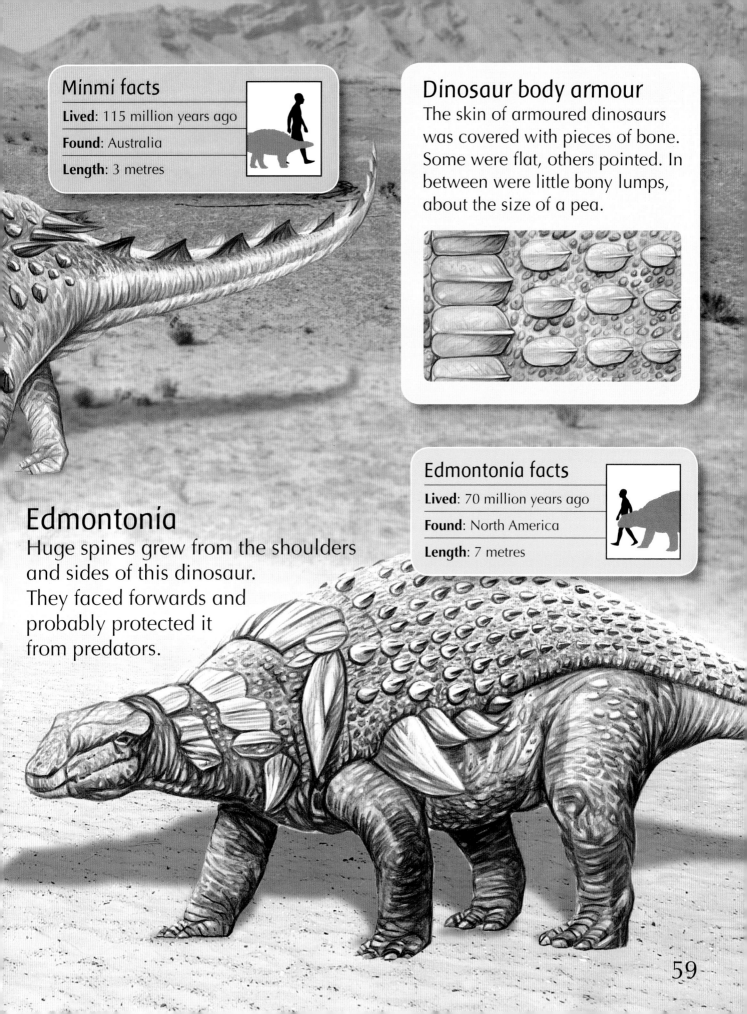

Minmi facts

Lived: 115 million years ago

Found: Australia

Length: 3 metres

Dinosaur body armour

The skin of armoured dinosaurs was covered with pieces of bone. Some were flat, others pointed. In between were little bony lumps, about the size of a pea.

Edmontonia facts

Lived: 70 million years ago

Found: North America

Length: 7 metres

Edmontonia

Huge spines grew from the shoulders and sides of this dinosaur. They faced forwards and probably protected it from predators.

Ankylosaurs

These armoured dinosaurs had a special weapon. An ankylosaur had a lump of bone like a club at the end of its tail. It could swing this against an attacker.

Euoplocephalus facts

Lived: 70 million years ago

Found: North America

Length: 7 metres

DID YOU KNOW?

An ankylosaur could break a tyrannosaur's leg with a blow from its clubbed tail.

Talarurus

Large bony spikes covered the back and tail of this ankylosaur. Like other ankylosaurs it had a heavy club of bone at the end of its tail.

Talarurus facts

Lived: 85 million years ago

Found: Asia

Length: 5 metres

60

Euoplocephalus

This dinosaur looked like a walking suit of armour. It lived in forests, and the dinosaurs may have moved around in herds.

Euoplocephalus even had bony eyelids!

Armoured head

An ankylosaur's head was broad, with a big beak for biting off mouthfuls of plants. Plates of bone covered the head.

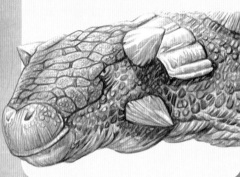

Pinacosaurus

This ankylosaur's head was only partly covered with bone. It lived in hot, dry areas of China and Mongolia.

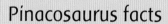

Pinacosaurus facts

Lived: 80 million years ago

Found: Asia

Length: 5 metres

Ankylosaurus

This dinosaur was one of the largest ankylosaurs. It had a big rounded body, shaped like a barrel, and was twice as wide as it was tall. Its legs were short but strong.

Body armour

The top of *Ankylosaurus*'s body was covered with thick plates of bone. Rows of big sharp spikes grew along the dinosaur's back, and it had horns at the back of its head. Only its tummy was unprotected.

Ankylosaurus skull

At the front of *Ankylosaurus*'s jaws was a wide, toothless beak. Further back were lots of small teeth which it used for chewing food.

Ankylosaurus facts

Lived: 70 million years ago	
Found: North America	
Length: 10 metres	

Warning sign

If attacked, *Ankylosaurus* hit out with its clubbed tail. Its skin may have blushed red as a warning sign that the dinosaur was getting angry.

Low feeder

Ankylosaurus had short legs and couldn't reach up to high branches. It fed on low-growing plants which it snapped up with its wide beak.

A tyrannosaur is wounded by a blow from *Ankylosaurus's* clubbed tail.

Ankylosaurus tail club

The heavy club at the end of *Ankylosaurus's* tail was made of two balls of bones joined together.

Ceratopsians

All ceratopsians had a parrot-like beak at the front of the mouth. They ranged from the size of a turkey to the size of an elephant.

Leptoceratops had a small bony neck frill.

Leptoceratops

This small dinosaur had a slim body and could probably move quite fast.

Protoceratops

A nest of fossilized eggs laid by this dinosaur was found in the Gobi Desert in Mongolia. The eggs were about 20 centimetres long and arranged in a circle in a little dip in the sand.

Protoceratops facts

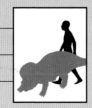

Lived: 80 million years ago

Found: Asia

Length: 2.5 metres

Leptoceratops facts

Lived: 70 million years ago

Found: Australia, N. America

Length: 2 metres

Dinosaur beak

Psittacosaurus's beak looks very like a parrot's beak. The beak was covered with a tough material called horn.

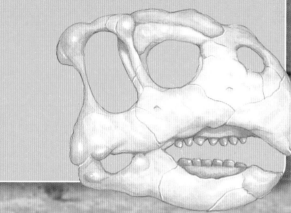

DID YOU KNOW?

Psittacosaurus means 'parrot lizard'. The dinosaur was given this name because of its beak.

Psittacosaurus

This dinosaur walked upright on its two back legs. It may have used its hands to gather plant food, which it cut through with its sharp beak.

Psittacosaurus facts

Lived: 130 million years ago

Found: Asia

Length: 2.5 metres

65

Triceratops

Triceratops is the most famous of the ceratopsians, or horned dinosaurs. It had three sharp horns on its head, and its name means 'three-horned face'.

Strong body

Triceratops had a big chunky body, short tail and thick legs. It weighed about 10 tonnes and was strong enough to fight off even fierce hunters such as tyrannosaurs.

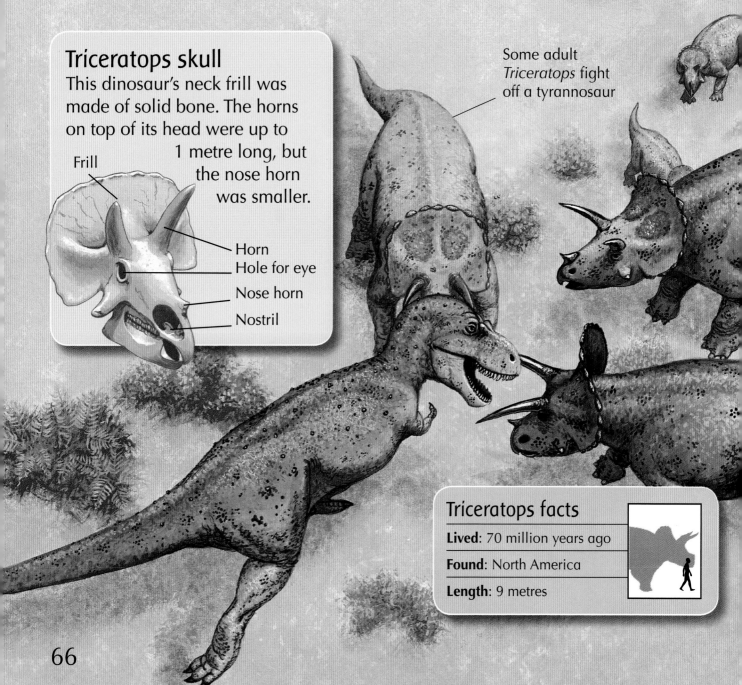

Triceratops skull

This dinosaur's neck frill was made of solid bone. The horns on top of its head were up to 1 metre long, but the nose horn was smaller.

Frill

Horn

Hole for eye

Nose horn

Nostril

Some adult *Triceratops* fight off a tyrannosaur

Triceratops facts

Lived: 70 million years ago

Found: North America

Length: 9 metres

Protecting the weak

Triceratops lived in a group, or herd, of animals. Young animals stayed in the centre of the group where they were safe from attackers.

Plant-eater

Triceratops looked very fierce, but like other ceratopsians it ate only plants. It bit off mouthfuls of leaves with its sharp beak.

Big battles

Triceratops probably fought over mates or who would lead the herd. They crashed their heads together and locked horns.

Pachycephalosaurs

These creatures are often called bone-heads or bone-headed dinosaurs. This is because they have a thick lump of bone on the head.

Built for speed
Pachycephalosaurs were probably fast movers. They stood upright and raced around on their long back legs.

Stygimoloch had lots of lumps and bumps on its head.

Stygimoloch
This is the only pachycephalosaur that had spikes on its head. These measured up to 15 centimetres long. Experts think that maybe only male *Stygimoloch* dinosaurs had spikes.

Stygimoloch facts

Lived:	70 million years ago
Found:	North America
Length:	3 metres

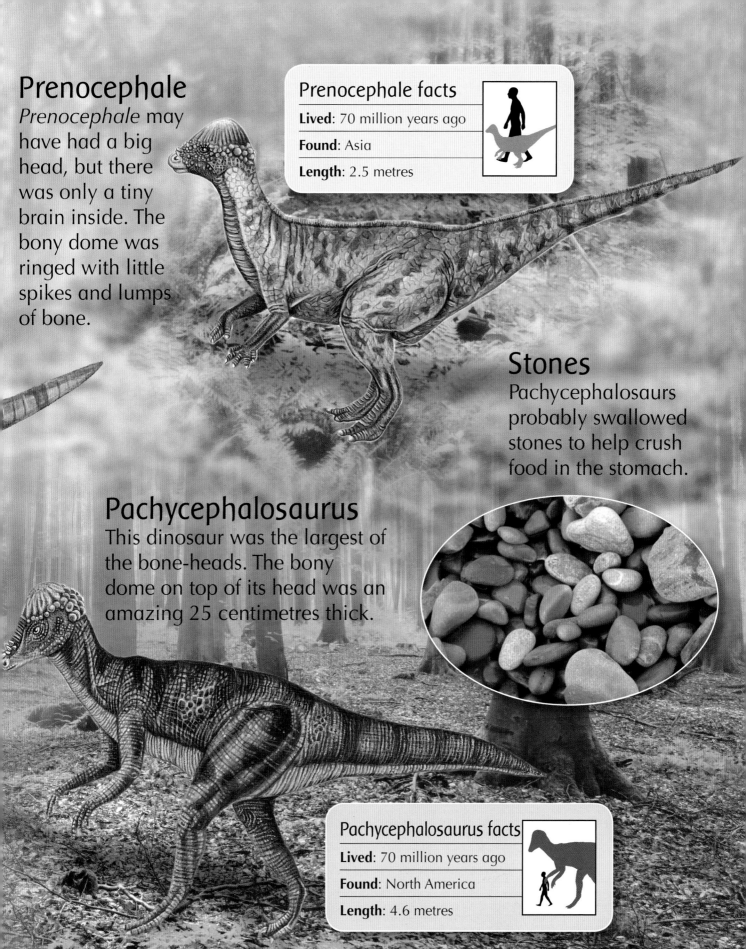

Prenocephale

Prenocephale may have had a big head, but there was only a tiny brain inside. The bony dome was ringed with little spikes and lumps of bone.

Prenocephale facts

Lived: 70 million years ago

Found: Asia

Length: 2.5 metres

Stones

Pachycephalosaurs probably swallowed stones to help crush food in the stomach.

Pachycephalosaurus

This dinosaur was the largest of the bone-heads. The bony dome on top of its head was an amazing 25 centimetres thick.

Pachycephalosaurus facts

Lived: 70 million years ago

Found: North America

Length: 4.6 metres

Stegoceras

These dinosaurs may have charged head on and crashed their bony heads together when fighting for mates or leadership of the herd. They may also have butted each other in the side.

Long legs, long tail

Stegoceras moved about on its two long back legs. It had a long tail, too, which it held straight out behind it. It had five fingers on each hand and five toes on its feet.

Two adult *Stegoceras* fight to decide which of them will lead the herd.

Stegoceras skull

The skull was up to 6 centimetres thick over the brain area. At the back of the skull was a ridge that was covered with knobs and lumps.

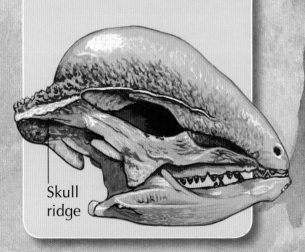

Skull ridge

Stegoceras facts

Lived: 70 million years ago

Found: North America

Length: 2 metres

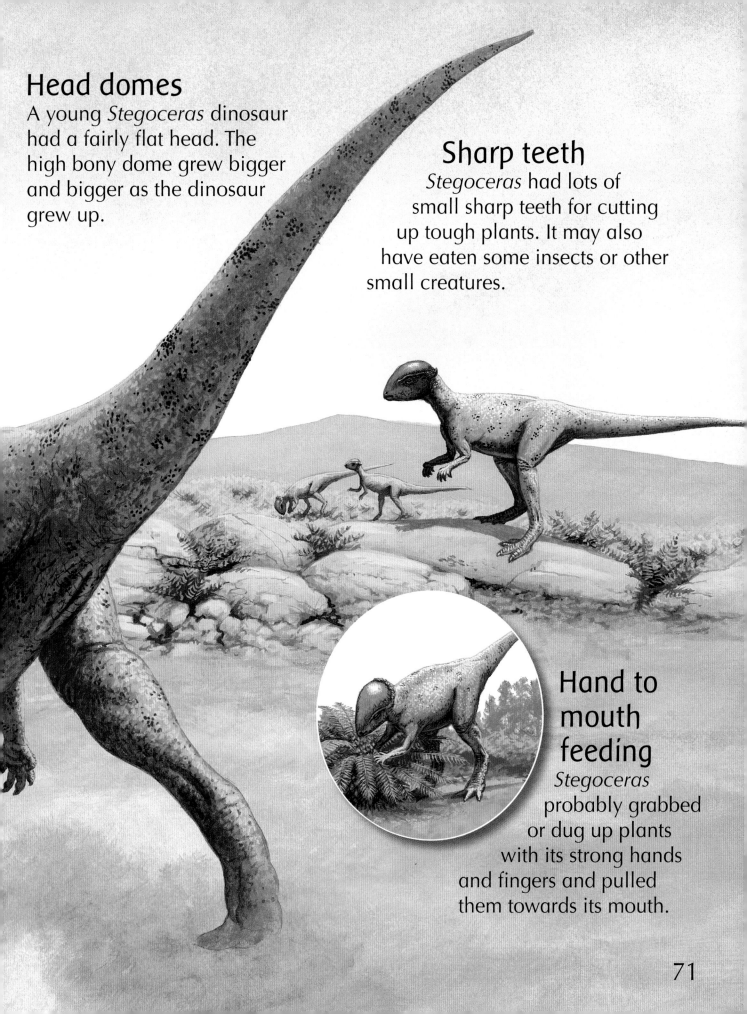

Head domes
A young *Stegoceras* dinosaur had a fairly flat head. The high bony dome grew bigger and bigger as the dinosaur grew up.

Sharp teeth
Stegoceras had lots of small sharp teeth for cutting up tough plants. It may also have eaten some insects or other small creatures.

Hand to mouth feeding
Stegoceras probably grabbed or dug up plants with its strong hands and fingers and pulled them towards its mouth.

Duck-bills and other dinosaurs

Many new kinds of plant-eating dinosaurs, such as duck-bills and iguanodonts, appeared in the Jurassic and Cretaceous periods. All had a bony beak for biting into plants and strong teeth for chewing.

Ornithopods – the 'bird-feet' dinosaurs

These dinosaurs are called 'bird-feet' dinosaurs because they walked upright and on tip-toe like birds. There were many different kinds of ornithopods all over the world.

'Different teeth' dinosaurs

These dinosaurs were also called heterodontosaurs. They had three kinds of teeth shaped for cutting, chewing and stabbing.

DID YOU KNOW?

Many ornithopods lived in big groups, called herds, made up of thousands of animals.

Parksosaurus

Different sizes
The smallest ornithopods were only about 2 metres long. The biggest were 10–20 metres long.

Iguanodon 10 m long

Hypsilophodon 2.4 m long

74

'High ridge teeth' dinosaurs

These dinosaurs were also called hypsilophodonts. *Parksosaurus* was an hypsilophodont.

Duck-billed dinosaurs

These dinosaurs are known as duck-bills because of their beaks, which looked very like a duck's beak. They are also called hadrosaurs, which means 'big lizards'. *Edmontosaurus* and *Parasaurolophus* were duck-bills.

Edmontosaurus

Parasaurolophus

Beaks

Ornithopod dinosaurs had bony beaks at the front of their jaws. These were covered with a hard material called horn. They were just right for biting off mouthfuls of plants.

Edmontosaurus

Hypsilophodon

Iguanodonts

The name of this group of dinosaurs means 'iguana teeth'. They got this name because people thought their teeth looked like those of iguana lizards. *Iguanodon* is the best known iguanodont.

Heterodontosaurs

These dinosaurs were the first of the ornithopods. They appeared about 220 million years ago and were all small plant-eaters that walked upright on two legs.

Three types of teeth

At the front of the mouth, behind the beak, were small, sharp teeth for biting. Then came two pairs of tusk-like teeth. At the back of the mouth were lots of wider teeth for chewing food.

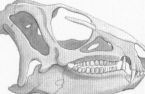

The strong tail was held straight out and off the ground.

Heterodontosaurus

Like most heterodontosaurs, this dinosaur had short arms and long, slender back legs. It was probably a fast runner. Possibly only males had the big tusk-like teeth.

Heterodontosaurus facts

Lived: 205 million years ago

Found: South Africa

Length: 1.2 metres

Abrictosaurus

This dinosaur had no long tusk-like teeth. It may have been a female *Heterodontosaurus* and not a separate species.

Abrictosaurus facts

Lived: 205 million years ago

Found: South Africa

Length: 1.2 metres

Dinosaurs with cheek pouches

As a heterodontosaur chewed, the food collected in its fleshy cheek pouches. The dinosaur then used its tongue to move the food back to its jaws.

Pisanosaurus

Pisanosaurus was one of the first heterodontosaurs and one of the earliest dinosaurs. Only some of its bones have been found, not a whole skeleton.

Pisanosaurus facts

Lived: 220 million years ago

Found: South America

Length: 90 cm (uncertain)

Lesothosaurus

Lesothosaurus belonged to a small group of dinosaurs called fabrosaurs. It was a plant-eater and had sharp pointed front teeth as well as bigger teeth for chewing.

Summer sleep

Two *Lesothosaurus* skeletons were found curled up together in a burrow. Experts think they may have crept in there to sleep through the hot summer months.

Small but swift

This dinosaur had long back legs and was probably a fast runner. Its arms were short and it had five fingers on each hand that it could use for grabbing and digging for food.

Low feeder

Lesothosaurus couldn't reach up very high so would have fed on low-growing plants. It may also have dug up plant roots with its hands.

A group of *Lesothosaurus* dinosaurs stop to feed.

78

Lesothosaurus skeleton

The body and legs of this dinosaur look very like those of a meat-eating dinosaur. But its head, bony beak and chewing teeth show that it was a plant-eater.

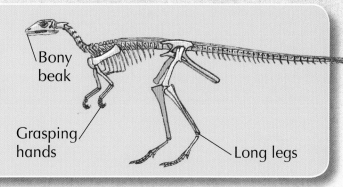

Bony beak

Grasping hands

Long legs

Dog-sized dinosaur

Lesothosoaurus probably lived in groups. The dinosaurs ran across the hot, dry plains of Africa, searching for food. A full-grown adult was about the size of a dog.

Lesothosaurus facts

Lived: 200 million years ago

Found: South Africa

Length: 1 metre

Hypsilophodonts

These dinosaurs lived like antelopes and deer today. They moved around in herds, feeding on low-growing plants.

Hypsilophodon

Hypsilophodon had lots of ridged teeth, and cheek pouches for holding partly chewed food.

Built for speed

Hypsilophodonts were fast movers. They could probably run at up to 40 kilometres per hour for a short time.

Horsetails

Hypsilophodon ate these plants. They first grew more than 400 million years ago and still grow today.

DID YOU KNOW? The biggest hypsilophodont was about 4 metres long.

Hypsilophodon facts

Lived: 120 million years ago

Found: Europe, N. America

Length: 2.4 metres

Fulgurotherium facts

Lived: 130 million years ago

Found: Australia

Length: 2 metres

Fulgurotherium

This dinosaur lived very far south. It may have moved north in winter to escape the icy weather.

Thescelosaurus

This was one of the last of the hypsilophodonts. It lived right at the end of the Age of Reptiles.

Thescelosaurus facts

Lived: 70 million years ago

Found: North America

Length: 4 metres

Leaellynasaura

Seeing in the dark

Leaellynasaura's large eyes probably helped it see well in the dark. This was very useful in the dark winter months.

This dinosaur lived in what is now Australia. At that time Australia was further south and was joined to Antarctica. It was icy cold and dark in the winter.

Asleep in winter
This dinosaur may have hibernated for some of the winter. This meant that its body slowed right down as it slept to save energy. It woke up when warmer spring days arrived.

Leaellynasaura dinosaurs may have lived in herds.

Warm-blooded dinosaur?
Most dinosaurs were cold-blooded so they had to stay in the sun to warm up. But *Leaellynasaura* may have been warm-blooded so it could survive in its cold home.

Built for speed
Leaellynasaura was about the size of a large turkey. It had long legs and could probably run fast. It fed on any plants it could find and may have dug up plant roots to nibble on.

Leaellynasaura facts
Lived: 105 million years ago

Found: Australia

Length: 1 metre

83

Iguanodonts

These dinosaurs lived like cows and deer do today. They moved around in herds and spent most of their time feeding on large amounts of plant material.

Camptosaurus facts

Lived: 150 million years ago

Found: Europe, N. America

Length: 6 metres

Camptosaurus

Like other iguanodonts, this dinosaur had strong teeth behind its sharp beak. It could even chew tough conifer needles.

Conifer forest

Conifer trees came before flowering plants and their needle-like leaves were an important food for dinosaurs.

84

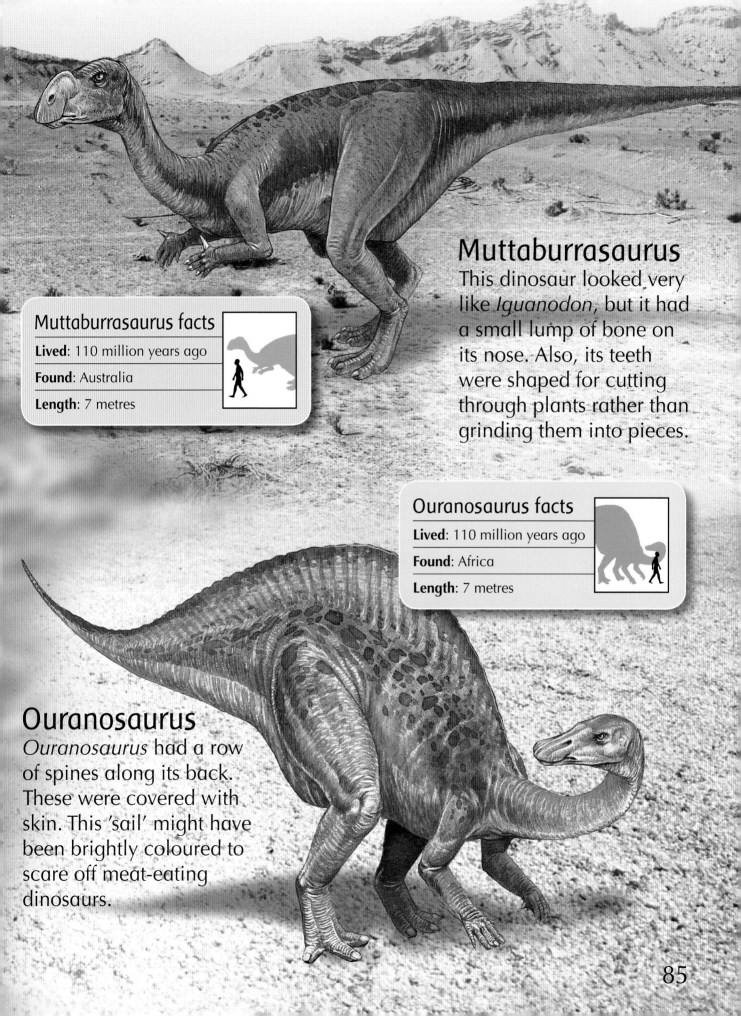

Muttaburrasaurus

This dinosaur looked very like *Iguanodon*, but it had a small lump of bone on its nose. Also, its teeth were shaped for cutting through plants rather than grinding them into pieces.

Muttaburrasaurus facts

Lived: 110 million years ago

Found: Australia

Length: 7 metres

Ouranosaurus facts

Lived: 110 million years ago

Found: Africa

Length: 7 metres

Ouranosaurus

Ouranosaurus had a row of spines along its back. These were covered with skin. This 'sail' might have been brightly coloured to scare off meat-eating dinosaurs.

Iguanodon

This was only the second dinosaur ever to be named. It was called *Iguanodon*, which means 'iguana teeth', because its teeth looked like those of the iguana lizard.

Horse head

Iguanodon was a big animal with a long stiff tail. It had a long head like a horse and its jaws were filled with lots of sharp teeth.

Two legs or four

This dinosaur could walk upright on its two back legs or on all fours. It could run at speeds of up to 20 kilometres per hour.

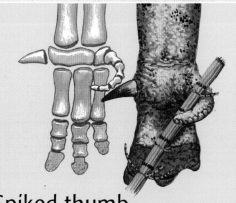

Spiked thumb

Iguanodon had four clawed fingers and a big spiky thumb. It could bend its little finger across its hand to help it hold onto things, such as twigs and leaves.

Ground to a pulp

Using the strong beak
at the front of its mouth,
Iguanodon bit off
leaves and twigs to eat.
It chewed its food for a
long time until it was
just a mushy pulp.

Using the thumb

Iguanodon could
have used its thumb
spike like a dagger
to defend itself
from meat-eating
dinosaurs.

Iguanodon facts

Lived: 130 million years ago

Found: Asia, Europe, N. America

Length: 10 metres

Hadrosaurs

These dinosaurs are also called 'duck-bills' because they have a beak like a duck's. They were one of the last types of dinosaur and lived until the end of the age of the reptiles.

Saurolophus

This hadrosaur had a long bony spike on the back of its head. This may have been covered with a flap of skin, making a bag that made the dinosaur's honking calls louder.

Hadrosaurus

A skeleton of this dinosaur was found in the USA in 1857. It was the first nearly complete dinosaur skeleton ever found.

Hadrosaurus facts	
Lived: 75 million years ago	
Found: North America	
Length: 9 metres	

Wide duck-like mouths

It's easy to see why these dinosaurs are called duck-bills. The beak at the front of the mouth was wide and flat. It was covered with a hard material called horn.

Saurolophus facts

Lived: 70 million years ago

Found: Asia, North America

Length: 12 metres

The head crest may have made the dinosaur's calls louder.

Lambeosaurus

Both male and female *Lambeosaurus* had bony crests on their heads. The males also had a spike of solid bone behind the crest.

Lambeosaurus facts

Lived: 70 million years ago

Found: North America

Length: 9 metres

Maiasaura

Nests and some fossilized eggs belonging to this dinosaur have been found so we know a lot about its nesting habits. The dinosaur's name means 'good mother lizard'.

Safety in numbers

These big plant-eaters lived in large herds of as many as 10,000 animals. They probably made their nests in groups, too.

Good mothers

Maiasaura mothers stayed near their eggs to protect them from predators. When the young hatched, their mothers brought them food until they were big enough to leave the nest.

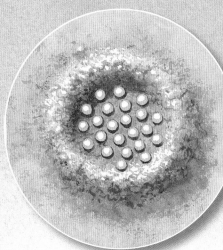

Maiasaura nest

The nest was a hollow in the ground and measured about 2 metres across. The mother dinosaur laid about 25 eggs, each about as big as a grapefruit.

At the nest site

Maiasaura was too big to sit on its eggs. It covered them with plants to keep them warm. When the young hatched they were about 30 centimetres long.

A *Maiasaura* keeps an eye on its nest of eggs.

Moving in herds

A *Maiasaura* herd had to keep on the move. Each animal needed to find as much as 90 kilograms of plants a day.

Maiasaura facts

Lived: 80 million years ago

Found: North America

Length: 9 metres

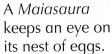

Some useful words

Ankylosaur
An armoured dinosaur covered with bony plates, knobs and spines.

Biped
An animal that stands, walks or runs on its two hind legs. Humans are bipeds.

Carnivore
An animal that eats meat.

Ceratopsian
A large plant-eating dinosaur with pointed horns and a bony frill growing from the back of its skull.

Conifer
A tree or shrub that produces seed cones, such as fir and pine trees.

Dinosaur
A reptile with an upright posture, not a sprawling one like a lizard.

Fern
A non-flowering plant with finely divided leaves called fronds.

Gastrolith
Stone found in the stomachs of some plant-eating dinosaurs to help them break down and digest vegetation.

Ginkgo
A tree that looks like a conifer but which sheds its leaves in the autumn. The only living species of ginkgo is the maidenhair tree.

Hadrosaur

A large plant-eating dinosaur with a wide, flat beak. Also called a duck-billed dinosaur.

Herbivore

An animal that only eats plants.

Horsetail

A plant with an upright stem and tiny leaves. Horsetails are related to ferns.

Ichthyosaur

A dolphin-like reptile that lived in the sea.

Iguanodont

A plant-eating dinosaur with hoof-like nails on its hind feet and spikes on its hands instead of thumbs.

Omnivore

An animal that eats both meat and plants.

Ornithischia

One of the two orders of dinosaurs. Bird-hipped plant-eating dinosaurs such as the ankylosaurs, ceratopsians and stegosaurs.

Ornithomimid

A fast-running, meat-eating dinosaur with a long neck and slender legs. Similar in appearance to a present-day ostrich.

Ornithopod

A two-legged plant-eater, some of which had crests on their heads.

Pachycephalosaur

A two-legged plant-eater with a thick skull.

Prey

The animal that is killed by a predator.

Saurischia

One of the two orders of dinosaurs. Lizard-hipped dinosaurs that include all theropods and sauropods.

Sauropod

A bulky, long-necked, long-tailed plant-eater that walked on all four feet.

Stegosaur

A large plant-eating dinosaur with rows of triangular bony plates on its back and spines on its tail.

Theropod

A two-legged meat-eating dinosaur, such as *Allosaurus* and *Tyrannosaurus*

Vertebrate

An animal with a backbone.

Index

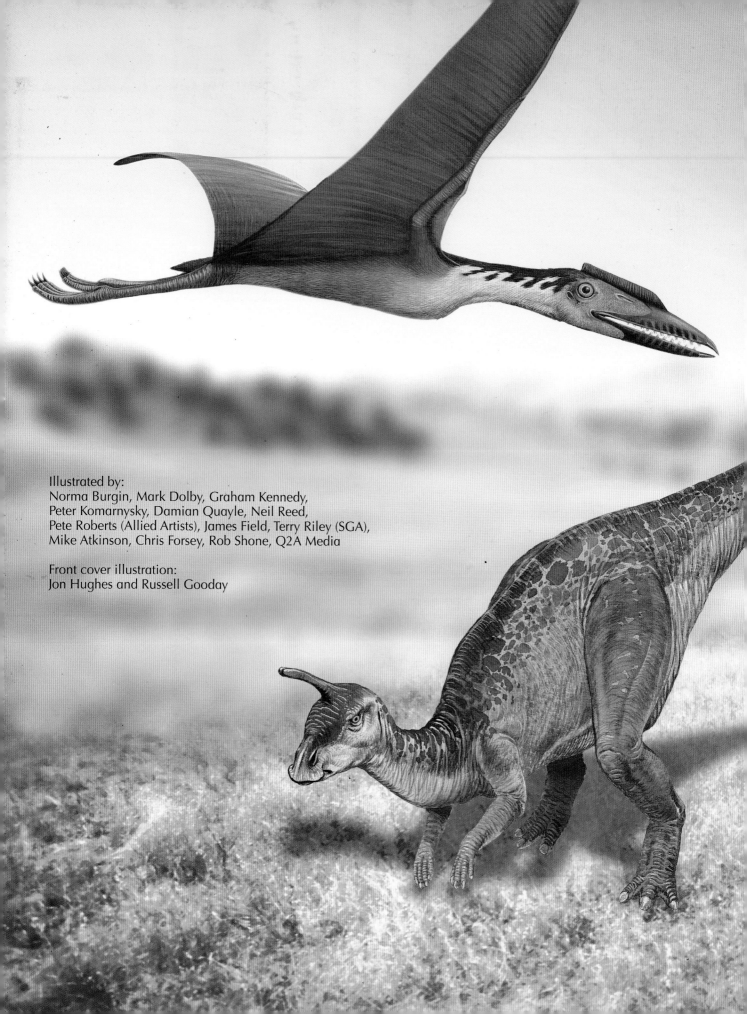

Illustrated by:
Norma Burgin, Mark Dolby, Graham Kennedy,
Peter Komarnysky, Damian Quayle, Neil Reed,
Pete Roberts (Allied Artists), James Field, Terry Riley (SGA),
Mike Atkinson, Chris Forsey, Rob Shone, Q2A Media

Front cover illustration:
Jon Hughes and Russell Gooday